From Reality to a Wealthy Place

Mone't S. Horton

HAKi -

Brother Thank You
for Your support !!!
Praying That You continue
to fulfill All that
God has placed in your
hands to do! Cheering
for You! Peace & Blessings!
Let's Go Higher,

Mone't Horton

ISBN: 1973756897
ISBN-13: 978-1973756897

DEDICATION

This book is dedicated to youth, women and men who are ready to face their truths and live a life of abundance and greatness as God intended. As I recount monumental accounts and shifts throughout my journey, it is my prayer that you can relate and know that you are not alone on your journey. The journey of life is not one that you just go through, rather one that REQUIRES you to GROW through. Knowing this, I challenge you to endure, stay in position and persevere.

This message is being read by who you are, but I am calling you forth to BE ALL that God has called and is calling YOU to BE.

This one is for YOU! Your destiny awaits... will YOU answer the call?

Mone't S. Horton

From Reality to a Wealthy Place

To My Songbird,

It gives me unspeakable joy to have nurtured and watched you evolve into a Amazing Leading Lady. You are my inspiration. All honor and glory to God for entrusting me to carry and birth an anointed vessel who has inspired, ministered and impacted so many lives. It has been an honor to walk along this astonishing journey with you. I pray that lives will be blessed, encouraged and inspired beyond measure to move to their "Wealthy Place".

Blessings,
Sunshine "Mama"

CONTENTS

ACKNOWLEDGMENTS

I am eternally grateful for the love, care and spiritual upbringing instilled by my mother, Evangelist Moniette S. Laury, grandmother, Pastor Carolyn Scott and great grandmother, Sarah Wallace. There is a host of women who have served as role models, mentors, guides and great clouds of witnesses in my life, far too many to list, but I am forever grateful, honored, committed and commissioned to carry on such a profound legacy.

From Reality to a Wealthy Place

Foreword

A Leading Lady is a queen who has not only overcome obstacles, but who has also moved from their reality to their wealthy place by growing from obstacles. Moving forward in life in spite of all, leading ladies understand that their current position is not their final destination.

Many call themselves leaders simply because they lived through a catastrophe. However, living through a catastrophe does not indicate that the person *lived after* the catastrophe. A person can physically breathe in air, soak in sunlight and release a dozen smiles, but be deceased on the inside. This type of lifestyle and living is not a wealthy place, but rather a place of destitution and potential self-destruction.

This is the very reason why this book and journal is so important. Mone't Horton is a living example of a Leading Lady who has not just lived life but has experienced greater in her life. She has taken an active stance to help other Leading Ladies overcome through her empowering prayer calls, presentations, positive social media posts and more. Mone't is sharing her voice further by developing this system to support Leading Ladies who are ready to take the next step.

I am honored to have been given the opportunity to support the development of *From Reality to a Wealthy Place*. In this book, you will learn what living a fearless life of abundance really is. In making your decision to step into your wealthy place, you will honor the queen within you. This book will allow you to better understand God's purpose for your life, which will lead to forgiveness of yourself, make you acknowledge fear and remind yourself that you have a purpose. This book addresses all of the necessary components of walking with confidence so that you can lead again, again and again!

LaQuisha Hall
Couture'd Confidence Coach

From Reality to a Wealthy Place

There was a power inside my mother that the world had not yet known.

1
MY STORY—A Retrospective View

"The whole 9 months your mother stayed sick. She stayed dehydrated and could not keep anything on her stomach. I had to keep feeding her...she was so light she looked like a ghost. At that time, the Holy Ghost spoke to me...He revealed to me that the enemy was trying to destroy you why your mother was carrying you. He said, BUT because you labored and prayed like Hannah I'm going to give you a healthy baby.

I had to tune everybody out, they were saying all kinds of negative things. I had to pray and trust God. Just me and him..."

- Pastor Carolyn Scott, Grandmother

It is my understanding that my mom had an extremely arduous pregnancy when carrying me. She was very sick, both visually and physically. It was so intense and bad that doctors and few family members alike were encouraging my grandmother to have my mother to abort me, simply let me go.

I can't imagine what that experience was like back in 1985, being faced with deciding to fight for your own life, or the life of the human being inside of you that the world hasn't yet known. I am quite sure that was overwhelming, coupled with the fact that she was young and had not experienced all that life had to offer.

As the story was told to me, during the same time my grandmother, Carolyn Scott was diagnosed with uterine cancer and had been going through the process of healing and recovery. In the midst of facing her own life-threatening challenges, she prayed, prayed like Hannah that God would be gracious to allow my mom to get through this life-threatening pregnancy to deliver a healthy baby girl.

Well, the rest is history, on August 17th, 1985, Moniette S. Laury delivered a healthy baby girl who I would like to say, has defied the odds with every breathe she takes and every single day God has granted her to live on earth. There was a power inside my mother that the world had not yet known.

****

What's wrong with me?

In my youth, I quickly learned that I was unique, different and set apart. I initially internalized my feelings and wondered, what was wrong with me? I had a few friends in elementary school. They smiled in my face laughed and talked behind my back—again, I asked myself what was wrong with me?

My mom would always dress me up, my hair was slayed in ponytails and curls— always made me feel like I was on top of the world! But, yet was something wrong with me? No matter how much I tried, I just did not fit in. I was short, chubby with my gap and although I don't really recall being made fun of and teased a lot, it was enough to make me feel like I was alone or that I didn't fit in.

During my middle school year's, I was still chubby, full-figured, but I came into my own. I begin to accept who I was rather than internalize what I learned to know as rejection. Instead of thinking that something was wrong with me, I began to accept that I was indeed different and unique.

I received the gift of the Holy Ghost during my early middle school year's. In retrospect, I know God has always been my saving grace.

If I had not found out that my identity was in Christ, as opposed to in what others felt and thought about me, I perhaps would not be who I am today. In receiving God as my personal savior, being baptized and filled with his Holy Spirit built my confidence. By the day my confidence increased and although at times, that feeling of loneliness and why are the cute guys not talking to me, began to creep up—I clung on to the fact that God loved me and was with me no matter what I was currently feeling and/or experiencing.

I recall the "Who AM I" poster board projects in school and I remember placing all the following adjectives on my ALL ABOUT ME web— *smart, intelligent, ambitious, serious, kind, nice, pretty, special, unique, sometimes nervous, brave, has courage, active, playful too and outgoing.* Again, these adjectives became affirmations to me that I held on to no matter what I encountered.

High school was next up and while I had confidence built through gaining a relationship with Christ, the reality which was my reality is that I would be dealing with a whole other dynamic of puberty and a sense of belonging. It was indeed another level. Again, I was coming into my own and did not quite know what to expect, but I braced myself.

I attended an all-girls school, Western Senior High School, *only the best*. It was a little intimidating initially, but I found a sense of belonging and community with my fellow doves, who caught the same bus as me to and from school, we were known as the "44 Bus Crew."

Throughout my high school year's there were indeed times that challenged me and I wondered if I was good enough. I always ended up back at my premise, clinging on to the fact that that God loved me and was with me no matter what I was currently feeling and experiencing.

On to college, WOW, it was finally here. The REALITY of adulthood and transition had come. Now, what am I going to do with my life? You know how we can pray to be grown, but when grown really comes it's like, ok, give me a little more time, PLEASE! So, yes, it was now my time, my REALITY.

Throughout high school I had an opportunity to take part in the Gilman Upward Bound program which assisted me throughout high school and my transition to college. I was blessed beyond measure to be selected as one of the recipients of the Granville T. Woods Scholarship at Baltimore City Community College (BCCC). That scholarship truly blessed my life. Through this scholarship, I connected with a genuine community of individuals who became family. There I learned the importance of networking and building long-standing relationships.

At this stage in my life, during my freshman and sophomore years of college I began to learn more and more about myself and what I wanted in life, at least based on where I was then. Based on where I was at the time, I had to make some crucial decisions regarding relationships and those who were in my circle. One major decision was to break-up with the boyfriend I had at the time. The first and only boyfriend I had ever had. That was a BIG move for me because I felt that we were on two separate paths—we were on the same page, I believe. In that season, I learned that sometimes you must love and care for some people enough to let them go. Holding on to them and trying to make things right, hinders them and ultimately hinders YOU.

I will praise thee; for I am fearfully [and]
wonderfully made: marvelous [are] thy
works; and [that] my soul knoweth right well.

Psalm 139: 14 (KJV)

Do you know that there is POWER within
YOU? Take a look back over your life. Have
you ever been made to think that something
was wrong with you? Or are there
relationships you need to let go? You were
indeed fearfully and wonderfully made. Now
is the time for YOU to embrace it!

Reflections

Now, is your time to reflect. Do some inner work. This space has been dedicated for you to **STOP, EVALUATE. ACTIVATE and ELEVATE.** Note to self: don't skip steps—there's an order!

EVALUATE (Unmask)—reflecting on the last passage, take inventory of where you are. *Commit* to facing the real you, dig deeper, lean in—there are some hidden treasures, pearls, resources etc. that you have not yet exhausted and/or tapped into. Write them here.

ACTIVATE (Tap-In)—now that you have evaluated, what *ACTION steps* are required to make sure you are *MOVING* towards manifestation and abundance? This can include short, mid and long-term goals, but you want to make sure that you are setting SMART (Specific, Measurable, Achievable, Relevant, Time bound) goals that you will commit to backing up with ACTION. Remember, it's all about you MOVING forward! Write them here.

ELEVATE (Manifest)—there are always areas in our lives and spaces around us that can afford us an opportunity to elevate— it is vital that we stay in a position to receive and take in all the goodness that is around us. But again, it starts with your mindset. In this section write down the *ELEVATION steps* that are required for you to remain in a position and posture of purpose. Rising above and choosing to go beyond! Write them here.

_____

_____

_____

_____

_____

_____

_____

_____

_____

_____

_____

_____

_____

_____

_____

_____

_____

_____

_____

_____

_____

_____

_____

_____

_____

_____

_____

_____

_____

_____

_____

_____

_____

_____

_____

_____

_____

_____

_____

_____

_____

_____

_____

_____

_____

_____

_____

_____

_____

_____

_____

_____

_____

_____

_____

I gained so much strength and
power over my hardened heart I
buried for so long...

2
THE COVERING

Growing up, my father, my dad was in the picture, but was not in the picture the way I desired him to be. I would always say, the girls with the girls and the boys with the boys. I was always hanging out with my mother and my brother was with my father. In my childhood, during my later elementary, early middle school year's, I believe, my mother and my father separated. That was a lot for me because while there was transition going on at home. I was transitioning to another age and grade level. While I was excited for going to the next grade, it was also all so terrifying.

Who would like me? Who would I hang out with? I was more conscious of my outfits...all those pressures that young people encounter when growing up began to hit me. My mom was always there to make sure I had all that I needed. And at the end of the day reinforced that I was beautiful and her big girl, so on and so forth. While my dad had a presence in my life, I honestly didn't get the paternal reinforcements that I thought I should be getting as a growing teenager.

He would always show up to pop his collar at graduations and celebrations, but he was not present during the major valley lows that I had to endure to get to the mountain tops of achievement. So much so, that as I grew older a void and sour spot grew in me towards my dad. I would still be cordial and hang out from time to time, but in the back of my mind and heart, I was like really? Are you serious? You have got to be kidding me...

I was never a disrespectful child. I learned to keep my feelings back within me until there were times of massive explosion. I kept it within. Which I know now was not healthy.

Into my high school years and college, the cycle of showing up when it was time to celebrate continued. There were always excuses of why he couldn't help with this or that and I was just totally fed up...
My mother shared my grief. Even as I sit here and type these words, I can recall and

feel the emotions that I felt in those moments well up in me. It was a hard time in my life. Don't get me wrong my father took care of the responsibilities of the household, but there were pockets of paternal voids that had been sprinkled throughout my life that had created within me a hardened heart towards my father. I am still talking about moving from your REALITY to your WEALTHY PLACE. See this was my reality. Into my college years, I struggled with this hardened heart. I went to church, continued with my life because it had to go on, but again, I had this hardened heart.

I had not realized at the time, but it impacted my relationships with the males in my life. Trust issues and not being able to take them for what they said they would do. After all, I had been let down so many times from the one person, the 1st male that I ever encountered—my father. I had feelings of not being enough—I'm short, I am overweight, I am this and that—simply put, not enough. Yes, these are feelings that I faced and of course life was still going on...

I never, ever had realized how much that hardened heart towards my dad had impacted my relationships with the opposite sex. I grew up in a family of beautiful, independent women who were confident in their own skin and did not wait for a man, at least as far as I could see to do anything for them. So, this was my experience, what I knew to be my REALITY—so I followed suit. I was not arrogant or prideful, but I was truly independent.

****

One day, during my college year's I was at my grandfather's house, packing up some items and God convicted me right on the spot! I had been reading my spiritual aunt, Annette E. Morton's book, *"Transference of Coverings—understanding the Role of a Man Over a Woman's Life."* As the title hints, the book brought to light the key roles, responsibilities a man has in a woman's life and their significance. In reading, I instantly had to confront the void of a close and authentic relationship with my father. Yes, I was blessed to have male figures in my life at church, school and at other points leading up to that moment, BUT I longed to have such a relationship with my birth father. I was totally thankful for the support of those men, but it never could fill that void.
The truth is that as I got older, took care of my business and attempted to burry my feelings, hurt and pain my hardened heart was growing too. It was not getting better, at all. As I continued to read the book, I was faced with this REALITY and knew that I

had to yet again, con front it head-on. That day in my grandfather's house, was the day that God took the cap off my pain and gave me a RELEASE. The one that I longed for... I was in the bathroom, looking in the mirror and tears begin to flood my face. I wept and I wept. I literally felt that with every tear God was draining me of all the toxins that advanced my hardened heart over the years.

First, as I stood there looking in the mirror, I had to **confront my REAL feelings**—no more denial, no more hiding, no more faking the funk on how I felt about my father. If I was truly saved and God was going to use me beyond my wildest dreams, I had to get over "this." It became less and less about my father, it was more and more about MY relationship with God and what He was doing, wanted to do and would do through me. I had to accept my father as a human being. Yes, he is human too. I had always pictured that a father had super powers and did super things, that he would be MY superman—and come down to save me from harm, wipe the tears from my eyes and be the first example of what a man should be in my life and how he should treat me. Well, that is not what I ever felt and in that moment, I had to dismantle the pedal stool that I had placed my father on.

Secondly, I had to **BE OK** with it. Be OK with the fact that my father was human and had faults, after all, we all do... that was not all, the other side of that is that his actions was a result of his experiences and exposure.

Lastly, in accepting and being OK with those truths, I had to then **manage my expectations**. For me, this was achieved by not expecting him to do any more or less than what he had been doing. In this realization, I gained so much strength and power over my hardened heart I buried for so long. My hardened heart was NO MORE. God had come in that moment and RELEASED me of the overwhelming pressure and burdens I had carried. It was not easy, but from that day to date, I have taken steps towards embracing my father for who he is and I have witnessed God during the rest in shaping and molding him to the man He wants him to be.

13 For if ye live after the flesh, ye shall die: but if ye through the Spirit do mortify the deeds of the body, ye shall live.
14 For as many as are led by the Spirit of God, they are the sons of God.
15 For ye have not received the spirit of bondage again to fear; but ye have received the Spirit of adoption, whereby we cry, Abba, Father.
16 The Spirit itself beareth witness with our spirit, that we are the children of God:
17 And if children, then heirs; heirs of God, and joint-heirs with Christ; if so be that we suffer with him, that we may be also glorified together.

Romans 8:13-17 (KJV)

Have you ever had a "covering" issue? Perhaps you longed for a closer relationship with your biological father or the male figure in your life? Or even wondered who would be there to take on that role in your life, complete your support system and uplift you? This moment and space is for you...

Reflections

Now, is your time to reflect. Do some inner work. This space has been dedicated for you to **STOP, EVALUATE. ACTIVATE and ELEVATE.** Note to self: don't skip steps— there's an order!

EVALUATE (Unmask)—reflecting on the last passage, take inventory of where you are. *Commit* to facing the real you, dig deeper, lean in—there are some hidden treasures, pearls, resources etc. that you have not yet exhausted and/or tapped into. Write them here.

ACTIVATE (Tap-In)—now that you have evaluated, what *ACTION steps* are required to make sure you are *MOVING* towards manifestation and abundance? This can include short, mid and long-term goals, but you want to make sure that you are setting SMART (Specific, Measurable, Achievable, Relevant, Time bound) goals that you will commit to backing up with ACTION. Remember, it's all about you MOVING forward! Write them here.

ELEVATE (Manifest)—there are always areas in our lives and spaces around us that can afford us an opportunity to elevate— it is vital that we stay in a position to receive and take in all the goodness that is around us. But again, it starts with your mindset. In this section write down the ***ELEVATION steps*** that are required for you to remain in a position and posture of purpose? Rising above and choosing to go beyond! Write them here.

_____

_____

_____

_____

_____

_____

_____

_____

_____

_____

_____

_____

_____

_____

_____

_____

_____

_____

_____

_____

_____

_____

_____

_____

_____

_____

_____

_____

_____

_____

_____

_____

_____

_____

_____

_____

_____

_____

_____

_____

_____

_____

_____

_____

_____

_____

_____

_____

_____

_____

_____

_____

_____

_____

Take out quality time, uninterrupted time—to converse with your maker, exposing your hurts, pains, faults, bad decisions, wins and victories.

3
THE SABBATICAL STORY

There was a pulling and a tugging, nothing seemed to be right. My spirit was vexed and I felt as if the weight of the world was laying upon my shoulders. I felt like this shouldn't be because after all I was doing everything right, going to church, giving all of my time, giving of my gifts, talents and monies— wasn't I doing the right thing? What else could be expected of me?!

I was in a place of spiritual dissatisfaction, Lord, why am I here? What is the purpose for my existence? What did you make me for? Because right now, I am not exactly sure if what I am doing is in alignment to my purpose and the predestined calling you have for my life—I mean the one that you talk about having before I was birthed out of my mother's womb—YES, Lord! That's the one, that one!

I was doing all the things that perhaps a good Christian is supposed to do, but had surely lost a connection to my CORE, my God—the One who connects and directs every piece of my life.

It was time for me to STEP away! I immediately arranged a meeting with my Pastor during the time and was RELEASED to my Sabbatical.

Sometimes in life you will just need to still away. Just you and the Lord. Forget about what others may say and do, it's during these times that you truly come into close relationship with God. Take out quality time, uninterrupted time—to converse with your maker, exposing your hurts, pains, faults, bad decisions, wins and victories. The fact is that He already knows, he just wants to see if you will be true to yourself and Him because He is the only one that can make it better.

.

¹⁰ Hearken, O daughter, and consider, and incline thine ear; forget also thine own people, and thy father's house;

Psalm 45:10 (KJV)

Is there a message that God is trying to get over to you? Or do you know what He is saying, but simply not doing? Taking the action steps? Perhaps you need some time to still away with Him. It does not necessarily mean that you need to be physically removed, you may just need to settle you mind, be renewed and adjust your prospective. It is vital that you take time to see what He is saying to YOU.

Reflections

Now, is your time to reflect. Do some inner work. This space has been dedicated for you to **STOP, EVALUATE. ACTIVATE and ELEVATE.** Note to self: don't skip steps—there's an order!

EVALUATE (Unmask)—reflecting on the last passage, take inventory of where you are. *Commit* to facing the real you, dig deeper, lean in—there are some hidden treasures, pearls, resources etc. that you have not yet exhausted and/or tapped into. Write them here.

ACTIVATE (Tap-In)—now that you have evaluated, what *ACTION steps* are required to make sure you are *MOVING* towards manifestation and abundance? This can include short, mid and long-term goals, but you want to make sure that you are setting SMART (Specific, Measurable, Achievable, Relevant, Time bound) goals that you will commit to backing up with ACTION. Remember, it's all about you MOVING forward! Write them here.

ELEVATE (Manifest)—there are always areas in our lives and spaces around us that can afford us an opportunity to elevate— it is vital that we stay in a position to receive and take in all the goodness that is around us. But again, it starts with your mindset. In this section write down the ***ELEVATION steps*** that are required for you to remain in a position and posture of purpose? Rising above and choosing to go beyond! Write them here.

_____

_____

_____

_____

_____

_____

_____

_____

_____

_____

_____

_____

_____

_____

_____

_____

_____

_____

_____

_____

_____

_____

_____

_____

_____

_____

_____

_____

_____

_____

_____

_____

_____

Sometimes by latching hold of
someone else's vision and
purpose you end up finding your
own!

4
A DECISION TO WIN WITHIN

One thing is for sure, winning is not only an option, but it is a conscious decision that one has to make and take steps toward. Before helping another to win and achieve greatness one must first look with in and ask the question, am I winning? The question is not only regarding the outward manifestation and possession of things, but is inclusive of one's ability to 1st and foremost win within which means conquering those internal, mental battles that many all too often fall prey to. The truth is that the outward manifestation and possession is only but a mere reflection and product of one's internal and mental posture.

In July 2011, I made a decision to face the fire—not only *my Reality, but the Real Me.* I asked myself—self are you winning? You love to see others win, but ARE YOU?

And if so, is it only outward? Or are you winning within? The type of winning that will supersede your goals, plans, skills and possessions. My answer was, NO. The truth is that I had accomplished a lot of things during that time at the age of 26, but I had not begun to work on the inner me which deserved more attention than what I was giving. My spiritual life was great, and my work life was flourishing too—so I thought until I hit a place of void and a valley of feeling complacent and all together stuck! Now, how in the world did I get here? I asked myself, I needed and had an urge to tap into something more, but did not know what it was or what it would be. I knew that I had loss the connection to my core, my purpose and the connection between God's plan for me and what I was actually doing.

****

In October 2011, after returning from an international convention, for my coffee business, coupled with a Women Who Win empowerment event in Houston, Texas, I was inspired to launch an Annual Leading Ladies Empowerment forum. I left the event both empowered and inspired to not only change my life, but the lives of people all around me, with a specific passion for empowering other women to win! I did not have all of the resources and answers to what, when and how this vision would unfold and prosper. All I did know was that it was God inspired with a sense of urgency!

I started the forum with my own funds, there was no budget and no sponsors. All I knew is that God had given me an assignment to complete and I had to move. For 2 years, starting in 2012, I hosted the Leading Ladies forum. One day towards the close of 2012, during the time I would have usually began planning the forum while sitting at my kitchen table after my devotions, God spoke to me and gave me precise instructions for carrying out the third forum.

It was NOT that easy for me, during this time, I was in my season of process, I had just left my place of employment to embark on this journey to find my purpose and what God would have me to do with my life. While I know he had come through before, I was super discouraged in the moment because I did not have any money to do what I thought needed to be done to have a quality event.

I immediately thought, where would I host the event? Who would pay for food and beverages? Décor? Giveaways? And all the other things that would take the event to another level—after all that is what we have done in prior year's, taken it to the next level.

In the following moments, I prayed, "God, if you have given me this vision, I need you to make sure that everything falls into place." I then released my concern of the "how" will it get done, embraced what He said and began to take action. I had my notebook in front of me and immediately God began to give me a download on the event theme, speakers and other logistics that I moved on. As he gave it to me, I took radical action. The amazing thing is that EVERY speaker he gave me immediately accepted the invitation without hesitation. I shared the vision with my grandmother, and she was able to secure a venue at no cost! Things were beginning to fall into place. I was in awe of what God was doing as I dared to go beyond what I was encountering in my

REALITY—daily reality. Despite of what I saw, I was moving from fear and learning how to activate and elevate my faith.

The 3rd Leading Ladies Empowerment forum was held on Saturday, January 18th , 2014. It was a great success with just about 100 attendees present. What would have happened if I choose to abort the vision God had given me? The women in that room would not have received what they needed in that particular season of their lives—without a doubt an IMPACT was made. I had no clue that many women, young and old, had been watching. The fact is that people ARE watching YOU and waiting for YOU to walk in YOUR total GREATNESS. Will you be resourceful and make a decision to MOVE? I have learned and promise you that once you make a decision to say YES, things will begin to fall into place.

Sometimes by latching hold of someone else's vision and purpose you end up finding your own! Who knew this would be birthed out of coffee!!!

"But God hath chosen the foolish things of the world to confound the wise; and God hath chosen the weak things of the world to

confound the things which are mighty" (I Corinthians 1:27).

Have you ever hit a road block? A valley? A place where YOU were just stuck?

No, it's not a good feeling, but one thing I have learned is that every low place is an opportunity to tap into the possibilities of YOU! I was walking around making grand plans for my life and self and neglected the fact that God had the Ultimate plan that I needed to align with.

Are you coming into alignment with God's plan for your life?

Sometimes we are trying to figure out why things are going crazy, buck wild and out of control and we really need to stop and ALIGN! We must come into alignment with His will and plans because they are perfect and lead to fulfillment of our life's purpose, destiny and allows us to manifest things that are beyond our wildest dreams and imagination.

Are you ready to face your reality? There is something so GREAT in YOU that the world still does not know! Can you make a decision today, to WIN? It's a conscious decision that we all have to make. It won't happen overnight, but a part of that decision is a commitment to embrace the process. Today, I encourage YOU to embrace your process, start from where YOU are and Make a DECISION to WIN!

The LORD is my light and my salvation; whom shall I fear? the LORD is the strength of my life; of whom shall I be afraid?
2 When the wicked, even mine enemies and my foes, came upon me to eat up my flesh, they stumbled and fell.
3 Though an host should encamp against me, my heart shall not fear: though war should rise against me, in this will I be confident.
4 One thing have I desired of the LORD, that will I seek after; that I may dwell in the house of the LORD all the days of my life, to behold the beauty of the LORD, and to enquire in his temple.
5 For in the time of trouble he shall hide me in his pavilion: in the secret of his tabernacle shall he hide me; he shall set me up upon a rock.

6 And now shall mine head be lifted up above mine enemies round about me: therefore will I offer in his tabernacle sacrifices of joy; I will sing, yea, I will sing praises unto the LORD. 7 Hear, O LORD, when I cry with my voice: have mercy also upon me, and answer me. 8 When thou saidst, Seek ye my face; my heart said unto thee, Thy face, LORD, will I seek. 9 Hide not thy face far from me; put not thy servant away in anger: thou hast been my help; leave me not, neither forsake me, O God of my salvation. 10 When my father and my mother forsake me, then the LORD will take me up. 11 Teach me thy way, O LORD, and lead me in a plain path, because of mine enemies. 12 Deliver me not over unto the will of mine enemies: for false witnesses are risen up against me, and such as breathe out cruelty. 13 I had fainted, unless I had believed to see the goodness of the LORD in the land of the living. 14 Wait on the LORD: be of good courage, and he shall strengthen thine heart: wait, I say, on the LORD.

Psalm 27:1-14 (KJV)

Reflections

Now, is your time to reflect. Do some inner work. This space has been dedicated for you to **STOP, EVALUATE. ACTIVATE and ELEVATE.** Note to self: don't skip steps—there's an order!

EVALUATE (Unmask)—reflecting on the last passage, take inventory of where you are. *Commit* to facing the real you, dig deeper, lean in—there are some hidden treasures, pearls, resources etc. that you have not yet exhausted and/or tapped into. Write them here.

ACTIVATE (Tap-In)—now that you have evaluated, what *ACTION steps* are required to make sure you are *MOVING* towards manifestation and abundance? This can include short, mid and long-term goals, but you want to make sure that you are setting SMART (Specific, Measurable, Achievable, Relevant, Time bound) goals that you will commit to backing up with ACTION. Remember, it's all about you MOVING forward! Write them here.

ELEVATE (Manifest)—there are always areas in our lives and spaces around us that can afford us an opportunity to elevate— it is vital that we stay in a position to receive and take in all the goodness that is around us. But again, it starts with your mindset. In this section write down the ***ELEVATION steps*** that are required for you to remain in a position and posture of purpose? Rising above and choosing to go beyond! Write them here.

_____

_____

_____

_____

_____

_____

_____

_____

_____

_____

_____

_____

_____

_____

_____

_____

_____

_____

_____

_____

_____

_____

_____

_____

_____

_____

_____

_____

_____

_____

_____

_____

_____

_____

I felt stuck and longed for so much more than what my reality served up on a daily basis.

5
A SEASON OF PREPARATION

One step, two step, three step, with each step I took tears began to flood my face. I tried to escape the tears in fear that someone was watching and would see, so I took bigger steps in hopes that I would reach my destination quicker. Finally, I reached the building... sucked up the tears and entered to the elevator and to the safety of my office. Boy was I happy that my office was at the front of the suite. I entered my office, shut the door, put my items down and all I could do is sit in my chair and weep. An overwhelming sensation took over my body and all I knew is in that moment something was changing, something far bigger than me because I had absolutely NO control over what was coming out of me. Where in the world had all of these tears been stored up for so long? What was feeding this endless river that flowed from my eyes to my cheek bones to rest on my desk where I laid my head in awe of what had overcome me in that very moment?

You see I had been praying for a change, looking for a change and searching for a change, BUT one thing is for sure I had no clue of the day, hour or minute in which it would come. I was at a stage in my life where I felt stuck and longed for so much more than what my reality served up on a daily basis. There was a void. A place that longed-for fulfillment. I knew it was available, but did not know how to possess it.

After while in my office, at my desk I attempted to start my day and begin to work, but tears continued to flood my soul. I then immediately realized that there was a RELEASE taking place, God was breaking me down...one by one he was removing the excuses, hindrances and things that would keep me from fully embracing the FREEDOM that He was calling me to in that very moment. He was settling in, and embedding in my spirit that HE had given me permission to experience the GREATER that I knew was available to me. However, immediately, I knew that it would NOT come without a cost! It would require FAITH and I would have to take the hugest leap and risk that I had ever taken. In that moment God had settled in my spirit that I would be leaving my security net—my 9-5. I had PERMISSION. While I had the permission and confirmation, He had not given me a time, BUT I knew with EVERYTHING in me that it was coming.

As I attempted to carry on, I received a knock on my office door...now how in the world can I open this door, eyes just about bloody read due to the endless tears streaming down my face—I couldn't hide it and make-up could not fix me up at this point! I cleared my throat and asked who it was, it was, OK, it was my Director—a relief I felt, but still I had to let it out...

She came in as I opened the door and I immediately let it out. Yet again, in that moment I was not in control because as the tears continued to run, I had to tell her exactly where I was and that I don't know exactly when, BUT I would be making a transition of a lifetime. Honestly, in that moment it was nothing that anyone could say to deter or move me from what God said, as he impressed and confirmed it in m y spirit.

From that day on, I had a new perspective on life—I knew with a new-found assurance that God had a purpose and plan for my life. Yes, there were times of uncertainty and disbelief, doubt, but I held on to His WORD and what He had did in me on that day. It was indeed a milestone and unforgettable step in my journey. He had gave me such a RELEASE and boldness about what HE said about little ole' me before the very foundation of the world. I had an expected end and HE was certainly in control. Not having a clue on the exact path and journey that laid ahead I clung on to every word He impressed in my heart that day.

What has God said to you? Are you holding on to something? Is it your time to RELEASE?

Reflections

Now, is your time to reflect. Do some inner work. This space has been dedicated for you to **STOP, EVALUATE. ACTIVATE and ELEVATE.** Note to self: don't skip steps—there's an order!

EVALUATE (Unmask)—reflecting on the last passage, take inventory of where you are. *Commit* to facing the real you, dig deeper, lean in—there are some hidden treasures, pearls, resources etc. that you have not yet exhausted and/or tapped into. Write them here.

ACTIVATE (Tap-In)—now that you have evaluated, what *ACTION steps* are required to make sure you are *MOVING* towards manifestation and abundance? This can include short, mid and long-term goals, but you want to make sure that you are setting SMART (Specific, Measurable, Achievable, Relevant, Time bound) goals that you will commit to backing up with ACTION. Remember, it's all about you MOVING forward! Write them here.

ELEVATE (Manifest)—there are always areas in our lives and spaces around us that can afford us an opportunity to elevate— it is vital that we stay in a position to receive and take in all the goodness that is around us. But again, it starts with your mindset. In this section write down the ***ELEVATION steps*** that are required for you to remain in a position and posture of purpose? Rising above and choosing to go beyond! Write them here.

_____

_____

_____

_____

_____

_____

_____

_____

_____

_____

_____

_____

_____

_____

_____

_____

_____

_____

_____

_____

_____

_____

_____

_____

_____

_____

_____

_____

_____

_____

_____

_____

_____

I could not give in to my
REALITY because I was headed
to my WEALTHY PLACE, but I
had to stay in position.

6
THE GREAT EXIT

Fast forward, approximately one year later, June 3rd, 2013, yet holding on to the RELEASE and confirmation God gave me...I found myself driving into work, no music playing, just thinking and, well, those uncontrollable tears began to run down my face again. What in the world could this be, I asked?

It was like déjà vu, that same moment came over me and that was all I needed. It was time to back up that RELEASE with ACTION. I knew then that my time was up in that particular season of my life—from permission to release to action...

I remember it like yesterday, I set in my car for almost an hour crying and speaking to my cousin sharing the confirmation that the Lord had brought full circle and settled in my spirit. I went on to carry on with my day, but every moment after felt so surreal. I went in, set at my cubicle, did work and wondered to myself, Lord is this truly what you want me to do? All day long, I went back and forth, back and forth in my mind, counting up the cost—questioning over and over, Lord is this really your will for me in this season?

Finally, it was lunch time, I had to run an errand, so I grabbed my things and headed out. While driving, I am still thinking, contemplating, praying and asking God to speak to me yet again and send a confirmation….How many times do we actually do that?

Well, I reached my destination and immediately God began to speak, I grabbed my notebook that I kept by my side and it was as if I had NO control. The Lord took over and I wrote what He said...

Today you make the decision and you make the right decision for you and your family. You will lead nations. You are victorious. You have me by your side—if I am for you, WHO CAN BE AGAINST YOU? NOBODY, SAITH THE LORD YOUR GOD. IF I HAVE BROUGHT YOU TO IT, I WILL TAKE YOU THROUGH IT. IN THE NAME OF JESUS. AND IT IS SO!!!

Season—STOP & SHIFT...Declaration of the Lord Jesus Christ—

NOW IS THE TIME. RESOURCES, CASH FLOW, NETWORKS of PEOPLE WILL FALL INTO PLACE BECAUSE I, THE LORD YOUR GOD HAS CAUSED IT AND CALLED IT TO BE. YOU HAVE BEEN SEPERATED FOR SUCH A TIME AS THIS SAITH THE LORD AND YOU WILL BE WHO I SAID YOU WILL BE, NOT WHAT MAN SAITH, BUT WHAT I SAY WILL BE YOUR LOT. GO IN PEACE FOR I AM YOUR GOD AND EVERYTHING YOU WILL BE AND NEED IS IN ME. AMEN.

In that moment, I did not need any further confirmation, with all of the FEAR of not knowing all the next steps, I knew it was NOW my time to fully ACT. If there was ever a time that I needed to have FAITH, it was

NOW because I was launching into the deep and going into uncharted territory. I felt like I was being stretched...

That day, I returned to my office typed up my letter and by the close of the week, it was official, I had given my letter of resignation.

My decision would not make sense to others and did not make sense to others— who would logically walk away from their livelihood, with a full mortgage, new car and other responsibilities????

***

In 2004, I walked through the doors of Johns Hopkins Hospital knowing that the skies were the limit for me. I knew that the opportunities were limitless and with hard work and dedication, I would be able to go from one level to the next. Well, my hypotheses was true. My work as an HR file clerk in a dusty file room was the launching pad to numerous opportunities to sharpen my skills, develop new skills and share my passion, gifts and talents within the world of Hopkins.

Who would have thought, who would

have known? Over the past 9 years, I have been privileged to "Live, Work and Grow" ... and be educated at an Institution that continues to make investments in the lives of individuals, one day at a time.

Today, I submit this letter of resignation at the most awkward of times, but I know if I don't let go of my present, I cannot embrace my future. In life we have the opportunity to take the circumstances handed to us or the opportunity to create the circumstances we want and are looking for. Today, I am making a decision and an investment in myself to embark on a journey to impact more individuals than I could ever imagine- one day, one step, and one beat at a time.

The most liberating feeling ever!

August 9th, 2013 I started a new chapter in my book of life. It was my official last day at my place of employment, Johns Hopkins Health System. For 9 years I developed skills personal and professional and built networks and relationships with individuals that will continue for years to come. But now, on this day I started a new track. While it was indeed a shift in the physical and natural realm, it was for me an even greater shift in the SPIRIT.

See, I was answering a call, a call that God had placed on my life long before I was conceived and formed in my mother's womb. It was a birthing of a legacy that's far greater than me, I am just a grateful beneficiary and member of such an awesome, start struck cast.

"Your Power Pledge"
By Lisa Nichols

I am unique. My journey has been filled with experiences
that have built my resiliency, defined my character and made me a better woman.
I am ready to cash in on my greatness, my brilliance, my God-given possibilities and my prosperity.
I will turn my valleys into my mountaintops, my obstacles into my opportunities, my test into my testimony.
I love my cinnamon, caramel, mocha and deep chocolate skin, my full lips, my round hips and my kinky hair.
I am a masterpiece of humility, gratitude, godliness and divinity. My beauty is real. My heart is good, and my

strength has been confirmed through the test of time with my mother, grandmother and great grandmother.
I will show the world how to treat me—and it's my job to give the world the best example possible.
I have turned my crawl into a walk, my walk into a run, and I'm now turning my run into my soar.
I am unapologetic about my brilliance, untamed in my quest to discover me.
I am no longer asking for permission to be me. I'm giving notice!

Yes on this day I received my wings in the spirit to go and BE all that God had called me to be. I was on a journey to pursue my purpose in the earth.

Now after all of the spirit talk, I was now faced with asking God what's NEXT? I made the MOVE, now Lord, what is NEXT? I stepped out now, Lord, WHAT IS NEXT??

My days were spent at God's feet, in total surrender because after all, my JOB was no longer, God had become the agenda and focal point. The inner work began and the search was on. For days and nights at a time, I stretched out in my living room floor crying out and asking God for direction sometimes to receive an answer, sometimes not and in other times to find comfort and solace in His Word.

I learned so much, in this season. The Word, had truly become a "lamp unto my feet and light unto my path." I spent so much quality time with the Lord, I believe that's all He truly wanted from me. He had to bring me close and show me a few things about me, so that I could be in alignment with his plan for my life.

I didn't see it all at the time, but my FAITH muscles were being built. It is easy to be good with life and all of its circumstances when all of your next steps are laid out and in view. However, it's another thing to be TOTALLY dependent on another for the very sustenance that is needed for you to survive.

You see I was that person that needed to know all the ins and outs, intricate details from beginning to end—I had to have the full scheme and layout in view. I needed to understand the setup, responsibilities, expectations etc. before I would make a move because I needed the results to be fruitful and be in control. This new chapter was not and did NOT work that way.

It was as if, I was given daily bread, straight manna from on high on a daily basis. God covered me and was so deeply gracious to me.

This season in my life did not come without worry, doubt, pain, despair, shame, feelings of loneliness, rejection or feeling ill equipped for purpose.

There was NEVER a time I looked like my situation. Yes, I can say that definitively. Every single mountain high and valley low had a purpose and was well worth it because it has brought me to this very point to pour into others what has inevitably pushed me to my purpose, with hopes that they will also live a victorious life. TODAY, I share with YOU pieces of my journey. It does not matter how many times I wanted to give in and throw in the towel, I could not give in to my REALITY because I was headed to my WEALTHY PLACE, but I had to stay in position.

Do you need to make a move? Let's GO!

Reflections

Now, is your time to reflect. Do some inner work. This space has been dedicated for you to **STOP, EVALUATE. ACTIVATE and ELEVATE.** Note to self: don't skip steps—there's an order!

EVALUATE (Unmask)—reflecting on the last passage, take inventory of where you are. *Commit* to facing the real you, dig deeper, lean in—there are some hidden treasures, pearls, resources etc. that you have not yet exhausted and/or tapped into. Write them here.

ACTIVATE (Tap-In)—now that you have evaluated, what *ACTION steps* are required to make sure you are *MOVING* towards manifestation and abundance? This can include short, mid and long-term goals, but you want to make sure that you are setting SMART (Specific, Measurable, Achievable, Relevant, Time bound) goals that you will commit to backing up with ACTION. Remember, it's all about you MOVING forward! Write them here.

ELEVATE (Manifest)—there are always areas in our lives and spaces around us that can afford us an opportunity to elevate— it is vital that we stay in a position to receive and take in all the goodness that is around us. But again, it starts with your mindset. In this section write down the *ELEVATION steps* that are required for you to remain in a position and posture of purpose? Rising above and choosing to go beyond! Write them here.

_____

_____

_____

_____

_____

_____

_____

_____

_____

_____

_____

_____

While I was going through the
process, I was learning to grow
through the process.

7
MY MONEY STORY—
TURN THE DOOR KNOB

As far as I can think back, I've always had money. Something was in my pockets. It may not have been the amount I wanted, but I've always had some money in my pockets.

Allow me to put that into context.

I grew up in a family of entrepreneurs, on both sides. Just about everywhere I could look there was a family member, my parents, grandparents, aunts, uncles and cousins— they had some type of business whether brick and mortar or within their home sphere.

So as a child, I quickly learned how to turn my gifts, talents and skills into profit. My mom owned a full service hair salon and boutique, so growing up in the salon I had a number of jobs. I cleaned, covered the phones, ran errands and, of course, I was the #1 shampoo girl. OH 'yes, I earned plenty of tips! I was so good that many of her clients would leave me tips even when I was not there. Quite naturally, I also picked up a few cosmetology skills and began to set my own clients and make extra money.

As a result of this exposure, I inevitably developed a business mindset. I was known for taking care of business.

****

As a young adult, in church, I learned the principles of paying tithes and giving offering. As I grew older and began to make my own money, I held tight to those foundational principles, not only given what was required, but going beyond when I could.

****

In college, I learned more and more about credit and the importance of keeping it straight. I was incredibly cautious and mindful of my finances and did not fall prey to any request to co-sign.

My friends would always call me a hustler, in which I would pay no mind because every time we went out, I had money in my pockets. I was found ready. I could always be found working and making my money. As far as I can remember—I've never had any bad feelings about money, I just always wanted to know how I could make more of it.

****

In 2011, I had a desire and need to create residual income. I was at a place where I just needed more beyond my 9-5. I thought that if I was to ever to fulfill the vision and dreams, I would have to enlarge my capacity and borders—it was not going to happen all within the confines of my bi-weekly pay. I knew so much more was available, I just needed an opportunity to make it manifest.

During the time, I was gun whole about making sure my credit remained intake, so I had my own system of managing my existing debts. I had purchased my home two years before at the age of 23 and was working to maintain my responsibilities. I needed an additional stream of income that would enable me to create more money to fund my goals and dreams.

****

One day I was introduced to a multi-level marketing opportunity. I was invited out to a meeting and of course eventually given an opportunity to sign-up. Initially I was a little skeptical because I was not sure if this would be the opportunity I was looking for. However, as I learned more, I was drawn to the company. Out of all of this, when it came to officially sign up, I did not have all of the monies to launch my business. The leaders worked with me to set up a game plan and within the next week, I had done the work to launch my business—*I was selling coffee.*

The rest is history! I worked, made some additional income and traveled on business for the next 3 ½ years through this opportunity. I learned so much during the time that I worked the business--even at times that the money did not come fast enough, I held on to my goals and the initial purpose for me launching my business.

I was growing, going beyond my comfort zone, facing fear in the face, meeting people and building networks. I was living large and in charge (lol)! So I thought. One day, I looked up and my once, firm, stable and manageable financial status was no more. I was now in a position where I had to consider bankruptcy or other options to remedy my financial picture.

After extensive research and receiving counsel, I realized that I did not need to do bankruptcy. Thank you Jesus, I said. But, I did need to make a move toward reconciling my debt and credit. I started to look at debt consolidation and decided to work with a company. I worked with the company for almost a year before I decided that they were not moving fast enough. Initially, I thought that they would be great because I would not have to face the dreadful conversations and questioning from bill collectors, but the process was too slow. So, I made the decision to close my account.

In making this decision, I did not make any drastic attempts to contact debt collectors to reach settlements. At the time, I did not have massive income coming in, so I did what I could with what I had, but my focus was really on making sure my necessities were taken care of. The thought of having to answer to debt collectors simply haunted me—how did I ever reach this point, I asked myself over and over and over. Not me! Why me! It went on and on.

During this season, God truly had me stilled away. While I was going through the process, I was learning to grow through the process. Having took inventory of my skills, gifts and talents. I learned to maximize on them and had multiplied my streams of income—I song, did hair, business consulting, started a consignment fashions line and enhanced my acting skills in a few plays. I was on the move. Tapping into the limitless possibilities of me!

2 Dear brothers and sisters, when troubles of any kind come your way, consider it an opportunity for great joy. 3 For you know that when your faith is tested, your endurance has a chance to grow. 4 So let it grow, for when your endurance is fully developed, you will be perfect and complete, needing nothing. 5 If you need wisdom, ask our generous God, and he will give it to you. He will not rebuke you for asking. 6 But when you ask him, be sure that your faith is in God alone. Do not waver, for a person with divided loyalty is as unsettled as a wave of the sea that is blown and tossed by the wind.

James 1:2-6 (NLT)

What are the possibilities of YOU?

Reflections

Now, is your time to reflect. Do some inner work. This space has been dedicated for you to **STOP, EVALUATE. ACTIVATE and ELEVATE.** Note to self: don't skip steps— there's an order!

EVALUATE (Unmask)—reflecting on the last passage, take inventory of where you are. *Commit* to facing the real you, dig deeper, lean in—there are some hidden treasures, pearls, resources etc. that you have not yet exhausted and/or tapped into. Write them here.

ACTIVATE (Tap-In)—now that you have evaluated, what *ACTION steps* are required to make sure you are *MOVING* towards manifestation and abundance? This can include short, mid and long-term goals, but you want to make sure that you are setting SMART (Specific, Measurable, Achievable, Relevant, Time bound) goals that you will commit to backing up with ACTION. Remember, it's all about you MOVING forward! Write them here.

ELEVATE (Manifest)—there are always areas in our lives and spaces around us that can afford us an opportunity to elevate— it is vital that we stay in a position to receive and take in all the goodness that is around us. But again, it starts with your mindset. In this section write down the *ELEVATION steps* that are required for you to remain in a position and posture of purpose? Rising above and choosing to go beyond! Write them here.

_____

_____

_____

_____

_____

_____

_____

_____

_____

_____

_____

_____

_____

_____

_____

_____

_____

_____

_____

_____

_____

_____

_____

_____

_____

_____

_____

_____

_____

_____

_____

What we think, we manifest.

8
THOUGHTS ARE TRULY THINGS

I woke up one morning completely energized and on a mission. In my new season, I was committed to taping into all my resources and possibilities around me and one had become—consignment. In 2014, I launched Mo's Consignment Fashions where I started with my own clothes—items I had in my wardrobe that were of course in quality shape and in many cases still had tags on them—*I am sure you may be able to attest?* So, I took inventory of what I had in stock and began this line in my home and then transitioned to my mother's salon to reach more clientele. Shortly after, I began to have private clients who had similar challenges, for a variety of reasons (loss of weight, transitions in style etc.), request that I take a look at their items and consign them on their behalf. I proceeded, did my business research, made the necessary appointments and their selected items were added to my consignment line. Of course, this was another stream and opportunity to *turn the doorknob.*

Consignment inventory was moving and I didn't do too bad considering that it was yet another stream of income created—passive income. As time progressed, my attentions were shifted to other business opportunities and less time was concentrated on moving consignment fashions. This in mind, inventory still piled up and was beginning to consume my living quarters. Oh no! This was not my intent, of course.

While I had other streams, my REALITY at the time was that all these streams including the consignment were working together to handle all of my financial obligations and necessities. It was bothering me that I literally had stock around me that equated to profits, but I was not committed to taking the necessary ACTIONS to make it happen.

Then on one magical day, I woke-up fully

charged and loaded, saying to myself TODAY IS THE DAY! I am gathering all this inventory, loading it up in my car and will MOVE it TODAY! In that moment, I began to take ACTION that began with a committed mindset—attitude, outlook, mentality to TAKE ACTION! My thoughts were aligning with my actions.

I made a call to my grandmother to inform her that I was heading down to her building to set up my consignment fashions. I was excited and energized and she quickly agreed, saying that she would call her building mates to get ready because I was on the way!

Inventory loaded, I was now on my way. I arrived in less than 30 minutes, entered through the back entry way and proceeded to set-up. Before I knew it, it was if building residents came from the NORTH, SOUTH, EAST and WEST!!! And they didn't come empty handed! I couldn't get inventory out fast enough because they were ready to purchase!

In less than 30 minutes, the majority of my inventory was gone and I had profited a little over $400! Needless to say, for the next few months I had scheduled certain days to be in the building with my consignment, on assignment!

In no ways do I mean or am I applying disrespect, BUT above I stated that I INFORMED my grandmother that I was en route—sometimes you will just have to give NOTICE, serve it UP and let others know that YOU have arrived. As I went on, I stated that she immediately agreed—NOW perhaps it was my EXCITEMENT & ENERGY?!—in business I have learned that NOTHING HAPPENS until YOU get EXCITED! Simply, what you put out in the atmosphere, you will, SHALL, receive in return.

NOW, what would have happened if I had not decided to take action? Make a move and simply get out of my own way?! Not sure, but one thing is for sure, I would not have made that money that day. This story has become an embedded staple in my journey, emphasizing that one's thoughts are truly things. What we think, we manifest. The more we think it, the more it becomes our reality.

How many times do our negative thoughts and mindset outweigh our positive ones? Can you imagine what can happen if one flips the script and decides to think on the positive that leads to limitless possibilities, rather the negative that leads to defeat and stagnation?

On this day, my whole perspective shifted. God knows I didn't feel like lugging all of those items down to my grandmother's building, but there was something in me just burning and wanting to take a chance. Well, it worked! It made me realize even the more, how much power we truly have inside of us. The thing is that many of times we get in our own way of success. In this moment, I CHALLENGE YOU to make a commitment to go beyond YOU. Do not get in the way of YOUR own success.

It's AMAZING how things begin to fall in line when you just make a conscious decision to MOVE...ACT! Radical outcomes are birthed out of radical actions. Sometimes you just have to surprise yourself and do something that is totally out of the box to get something totally beyond your expectations.

Reflections

Now, is your time to reflect. Do some inner work. This space has been dedicated for you to **STOP, EVALUATE. ACTIVATE and ELEVATE.** Note to self: don't skip steps—there's an order!

EVALUATE (Unmask)—reflecting on the last passage, take inventory of where you are. *Commit* to facing the real you, dig deeper, lean in—there are some hidden treasures, pearls, resources etc. that you have not yet exhausted and/or tapped into. Write them here.

ACTIVATE (Tap-In)—now that you have evaluated, what *ACTION steps* are required to make sure you are *MOVING* towards manifestation and abundance? This can include short, mid and long-term goals, but you want to make sure that you are setting SMART (Specific, Measurable, Achievable, Relevant, Time bound) goals that you will commit to backing up with ACTION. Remember, it's all about you MOVING forward! Write them here.

ELEVATE (Manifest)—there are always areas in our lives and spaces around us that can afford us an opportunity to elevate— it is vital that we stay in a position to receive and take in all the goodness that is around us. But again, it starts with your mindset. In this section write down the *ELEVATION steps* that are required for you to remain in a position and posture of purpose? Rising above and choosing to go beyond! Write them here.

_____

_____

_____

_____

_____

_____

_____

_____

_____

_____

_____

_____

_____

_____

_____

_____

_____

_____

_____

_____

_____

_____

_____

_____

_____

_____

_____

_____

_____

_____

_____

There was grace and a covering
in every place I found myself in—
only God could have done that.

9
LIGHTS OUT

Early on a Saturday morning in 2015, I was getting prepared to meet a client in my home. I began to prepare and in one split moment I found myself in the dark. The sun was shining through my basement window, I used it as I sought to find out what was going on. I went to my electric box—it wasn't that. I peeked outside to see if there perhaps was a neighborhood blackout—nope, it wasn't that either. AND then it hit me—my utilities had been cut off. My season of overflowing grace had come to an end. I immediately called the utility company and, yes, it was confirmed, my lights had been shut off. Now how in the world am I supposed to conduct business under these circumstances—HOW EMBARASSING!!!

In that moment, I was consumed with overwhelming emotions because I had NEVER been in this type of situation. A flood of tears rushed down my face, as a herd of thoughts went through my mind. That light shining through my window was no more—I felt like I was in a dark space and there was no escape. I was in a low place, sinking even further by the second. How could God allow me to be in such a low place? I thought He loved me? I thought He cared? Right? Now, God, where are you right now?! It was NOT supposed to go this far?!!! I've followed your instructions AND you allow this to happen?!!!

In that moment, all of these thoughts consumed my mind. I was definitely done! You could stick a fork in me! Thankfully, I had a dear friend with me who did NOT allow me to drown in the moment. As I recall this very story, I am so grateful that my friend was by my side. In the moment I started crying and he immediately said, "No, you're going to pull yourself together and take care of your business! You are strong and everything is going to work out." He wiped the tears from my eyes, I sucked up the rest and went to action. I called my client and let her know that there would be an adjustment in the location.

Next, I tapped into local resources for assistance. After several calls I was thankfully able to reach someone who immediately informed me of what I needed to do. I had to come up with a portion of the funding to reconcile my account and the remaining balance was covered by the local assistance programming. I camped out one night in the dark and within the next day my services were restored.

Yes, I could have went to any family member's house and of course my mothers and grandmothers; however, I needed to endure this step in my process. It was hard, but I choose not to escape—my faith and endurance muscles were being built and I had to stay in position. Sometimes our pride does not allow us to feel and be human. There was grace and a covering in every place I found myself in—only God could have done that.

31 "So don't worry about these things, saying, 'What will we eat? What will we drink? What will we wear?' 32 These things dominate the thoughts of unbelievers, but your heavenly Father already knows all your needs. 33 Seek the Kingdom of God[a] above all else, and live righteously, and he will give you everything you need.

34 "So don't worry about tomorrow, for tomorrow will bring its own worries. Today's trouble is enough for today.

Matthew 6:31-34 (NLT)

Are you trying to escape your process? STOP, remember there is an order! The process is REQUIRED! Don't just go through, but choose to grow through.

Reflections

Now, is your time to reflect. Do some inner work. This space has been dedicated for you to **STOP, EVALUATE. ACTIVATE and ELEVATE.** Note to self: don't skip steps—there's an order!

EVALUATE (Unmask)—reflecting on the last passage, take inventory of where you are. *Commit* to facing the real you, dig deeper, lean in—there are some hidden treasures, pearls, resources etc. that you have not yet exhausted and/or tapped into. Write them here.

ACTIVATE (Tap-In)—now that you have evaluated, what *ACTION steps* are required to make sure you are *MOVING* towards manifestation and abundance? This can include short, mid and long-term goals, but you want to make sure that you are setting SMART (Specific, Measurable, Achievable, Relevant, Time bound) goals that you will commit to backing up with ACTION. Remember, it's all about you MOVING forward! Write them here.

ELEVATE (Manifest)—there are always areas in our lives and spaces around us that can afford us an opportunity to elevate— it is vital that we stay in a position to receive and take in all the goodness that is around us. But again, it starts with your mindset. In this section write down the *ELEVATION steps* that are required for you to remain in a position and posture of purpose? Rising above and choosing to go beyond! Write them here.

_____

_____

_____

_____

_____

_____

_____

_____

_____

_____

_____

_____

Face your money story. Leave
denial behind. Embrace, evaluate
and commit to reconciliation.

10
ON A MISSION

I had to face my debt and bill collectors head-on. The thought of their bad attitudes absolutely gave me the blues. At times, I actually felt like it was them I owed the money to.

In fact, I recall one in particular that proceeded to tell me, "no one should have to send you letters on debt and monies you know you were loaned and received...not to mention that several letters were sent." It took a whole lot of Jesus and prayers on that phone "that" day because I had to remind her that, "ma'am" I am the one who called you to reconcile my account. Please do not act as if you dotted every "I" and crossed every "T" in your life, she replied, "we are not talking about ME, we're talking about YOU." Again, I called on JESUS!!!... I was appalled!!!In that moment, I took several breathes, so that I would not go outside of myself. I had to remember my MISSION. After several breaths, inhales and exhales we both got it together and came to a settlement as if WE were best friends. I tell you, again, you have to face your debt HEAD-ON. LITERALLY.

In your money story you become absolutely vulnerable. Wide open—almost necked. While there is certainly an obligation to "pay," people must learn to handle others with care because they don't know who and whose you are and they sure enough don't know your story!!! It takes a lot to get it all together and face your debt, BUT it is all so refreshing to TURN the DOOR KNOB! It's a part of manifesting!

.

⁷ For God hath not given us the spirit of fear; but of power, and of love, and of a sound mind.

2 Timothy 1:7 (KJV)

Face your money story. Leave denial behind. Embrace, evaluate and commit to reconciliation.

***

Many people want to rain with Him, but very few are willing to suffer. They want God to hand out the blessings, but don't want to do any work. The word of God says, *"if we suffer, we shall also reign with him: if we deny him, he also will deny us... (2 Timothy 2:12)."* I've learned that it does not work like that. We must learn how to "suffer" go through and not only go through, but GROW through.

In doing so, YOU have to REACH for it! This means digging into the resources surrounding you. Everything is NOT going to be handed to you on a silver platter. So, I had to do my due diligence and research to find resources. It is important to learn how to navigate the valley—the low places in life.

There are supports and resources ALL around you. You have to put YOUR pride away and tap in, evaluate, so that you activate and elevate above your current situation—your REALITY.

In this season, I had to know with certainty that God was NOT going to put any more on me than what I could bear. It did not feel good at the time, but I had to pull up my boot straps, put my bigger draws ON and Jump in—all IN!

After all, faith without works is dead! And I like to add, dead as a door knob!

You see we deal with door knobs every day, they are the gateway, entry and exit that allows us to get from one place to the next. If we do not turn the door knob, we cannot get to the next place, position or destination. Except on the occasions that someone will be kind and open the door for us—that's favor; however others may provide automatic access. Otherwise, we have to do some physical work, place our hand on the knob and TURN. Yes, even the door knob you must reach for!

If you don't reach for it, you won't get to your next destination—it connects you to YOUR NEXT. The situation you are in is a part of where you are going—it is necessary—what I call a necessary season—don't allow it to be wasted. God doesn't allow anything that we go through to be wasted. It is up to us to acknowledge that truth. Then and only then will we not go through, but we will GROW through every valley low and persevere to live a life of purpose.

Reflections

Now, is your time to reflect. Do some inner work. This space has been dedicated for you to **STOP, EVALUATE. ACTIVATE and ELEVATE.** Note to self: don't skip steps—there's an order!

EVALUATE (Unmask)—reflecting on the last passage, take inventory of where you are. *Commit* to facing the real you, dig deeper, lean in—there are some hidden treasures, pearls, resources etc. that you have not yet exhausted and/or tapped into. Write them here.

ACTIVATE (Tap-In)—now that you have evaluated, what *ACTION steps* are required to make sure you are *MOVING* towards manifestation and abundance? This can include short, mid and long-term goals, but you want to make sure that you are setting SMART (Specific, Measurable, Achievable, Relevant, Time bound) goals that you will commit to backing up with ACTION. Remember, it's all about you MOVING forward! Write them here.

ELEVATE (Manifest)—there are always areas in our lives and spaces around us that can afford us an opportunity to elevate— it is vital that we stay in a position to receive and take in all the goodness that is around us. But again, it starts with your mindset. In this section write down the *ELEVATION steps* that are required for you to remain in a position and posture of purpose? Rising above and choosing to go beyond! Write them here.

_____

_____

_____

_____

_____

_____

_____

_____

_____

_____

_____

11
CONCLUSION:
A WEALTHY PLACE

The Wealthy Place is all about "mindset maintenance." It places very little emphasizes on the external things happening in one's life or to them at a particular time (One's "Reality"), but rather places focus on the things that are happening internally (one's own thoughts and perspective(s)). This is where it all starts and must be in direct relation (and relationship) to one's core—that is where Jesus is—He is the center, the nucleus of everything.

A Season of Rest

This is your season to take "rest" said the Lord. I asked myself, what did this actually mean? And what does it specifically mean, as it pertained to me and what God was saying? I had grown accustomed to always moving, doing and above all taking care of my business. But, again, God in His own way had been impressing upon me that I needed to REST.

So, in my studies and quiet time, I sought to see what He was saying to me. I started by defining the word rest. *As a verb, I found that it meant (1) to cease from work, refresh and recover your strength; (2) it meant to be positioned, to be placed and be supported by—as in to stay in a specified position. As a noun, it could be considered a period of time and/or instance or as an object used to support something. Some examples may include—a stand, shelf, base, rack, holder or frame.*

Sometimes rest meant—mentally, resting in my thoughts etc. and at other times it meant to rest from physical labor, to actually be still. In this season I had to be attentive to what God was doing and how He was moving because I wanted to be in alignment with what he was saying and what rest I should be employing.

Hebrews 4:1-10 (NLT)
Promised Rest for God's People

4 God's promise of entering his rest still stands, so we ought to tremble with fear that some of you might fail to experience it. ² For this good news—that God has prepared this rest—has been announced to us just as it was to them. But it did them no good because they didn't share the faith of those who listened to God. ³ For only we who believe can enter his rest. As for the others, God said,

"In my anger I took an oath:

'They will never enter my place of rest,'"¹ even though this rest has been ready since he made the world. ⁴ We know it is ready because of the place in the Scriptures where it mentions the seventh day: "On the seventh day God rested from all his work."¹⁵ But in the other passage God said, "They will never enter my place of rest."

⁶ So God's rest is there for people to enter, but those who first heard this good news failed to enter because they disobeyed God. ⁷ So God set another time for entering his rest, and that time is today. God announced this through David much later in the words already quoted:

*"Today when you hear his voice,
don't harden your hearts."[e]*
*8 Now if Joshua had succeeded in giving
them this rest, God would not have spoken
about another day of rest still to come. 9 So
there is a special rest[f] still waiting for the
people of God. 10 For all who have entered
into God's rest have rested from their labors,
just as God did after creating the world.*

In reflecting on this passage, I concluded
that if physical rest is important to our
physical well-being, spiritual rest is even
more important to our spiritual well-being.
For me this meant that I needed to take
inventory and make sure that I was giving
God the time that He required of me. I mean
quality time. Time that was not interrupted
and spent going down my list of wants, needs
and request.

In addition, I resolved that to truly
"enter into" a place or position of rest, there
must be a "release" or "relinquishing of"
control, pride and leaning on one's own or an
individual's abilities to replace, transition,
transfer belief, trust, obedience, authority
and confidence in another being. I had to
truly let go and totally surrender my will to

His will.

How do I Rest?

1. ***Stay Connected***—to him and be in relationship with him, coupled with surrounding yourself with likeminded people.
2. ***Stay in Position***—Be still, don't wave and wonder. Stand firm on the promises of God—Stop wandering. Allow your thoughts to take root and be grounded in His Word that your faith and belief grow in Him!
3. ***Stay Inspired***—believe and receive. Go back to what He said in the 1st place. Remind yourself. Write the vision and make it plain.
4. ***Stay FOCUSED***—know that God has a plan. Be committed to follow the course that he has placed YOU on—come what may. Be still and rest in God. Stop giving unappreciative people what God has given to you. Everyone does not appreciate things like you. You have to leave them to God and allow them to grow up and learn the lesson that God is trying to teach them. Stop getting in the way!

A Promise Made is a Promise Kept

The Call of Abram

12 The LORD had said to Abram, "Leave your native country, your relatives, and your father's family, and go to the land that I will show you. ²I will make you into a great nation. I will bless you and make you famous, and you will be a blessing to others.

Genesis 12:1-2 (NLT)

Throughout my journey, I found myself in the Word of God. I particularly identified with the story of Abram who became Abraham and God's Promise to him. God made a promise to him that slowly and unseeingly unraveled over the course of years. So much, so that Abraham literally had to walk with God. Though God had made a promise, he yet and still had to endure the process. At times, he even got above himself, asked questions and laughed in disbelief that God would still follow through and deliver on His Word. He went from one encounter to the next setting up an alter in reverence to God for every victory won. He had to gird up his loins all the way. God sent him little reminders along the way, he took his word and stayed in position.

Abram Is Named Abraham

17 When Abram was ninety-nine years old, the LORD appeared to him and said, "I am El-Shaddai—'God Almighty.' Serve me faithfully and live a blameless life. *2 I will make a covenant with you, by which I will guarantee to give you countless descendants."*

3 At this, Abram fell face down on the ground. Then God said to him, 4 "This is my covenant with you: I will make you the father of a multitude of nations! 5 What's more, I am changing your name. It will no longer be Abram. Instead, you will be called Abraham, for you will be the father of many nations. 6 I will make you extremely fruitful. Your descendants will become many nations, and kings will be among them!

7 "I will confirm my covenant with you and your descendants after you, from generation to generation. This is the everlasting covenant: I will always be your God and the God of your descendants after you. 8 And I will give the entire land of Canaan, where you now live as a foreigner, to you and your descendants. It will be their possession forever, and I will be their God."

~

Have you ever been left with a word or promise from God? What did you do? What will you commit to doing differently? I had to remind myself over and over, that a promise made by God is indeed a promise kept. NOW, I am living in the promise.

***

This year will be different, my daughter. Rest in me. You will not have to work hard as you have. My promises and favor will be manifested in your life and will overtake you like NEVER, EVER BEFORE. Thus saith, the Lord of Host. I am with you as I have always been right by your side. Trust and believe me when I say, It is Manifestation Time. Amen.

- What God gave me, January 3, 2015

Say Yes

Sometimes in our journeys we start and try to wonder and figure out how we are going to get to the next step, the next place, the next position. Then after a while, we turn around, look up and realize the place that we are in is so far ahead than when we first started. I've learned, the avenue in which we use to get to the place where we need to go, takes care of its self, but what's most important in the process is our commitment to say yes to manifest our dreams and make them our reality. Once you say yes, make the conscious decision, commit to you and the process, journey and to whatever the plan, destiny, purpose God has set before you, the stages, the steps, the ways and the means begin to unfold before you. BUT you must first say yes. Yes... yes, yes... I will go, yes, I will lead, yes I will stay in position, yes I will stand, yes I will believe, yes I will... I will be, I will stand in my greatness, I will stand in victory, I will stand in faith, I will stand in hope, I will stand in belief in spite of what I see. I will be, I will be all that God has called and calling me to be. It doesn't matter your past or your family situation. The only thing that matters is your "YES." The only thing that separates you from the rest is your yes. Your willingness to commit to the process. Your willingness to endure. Your willingness not to be selfish because there are individuals behind you, waiting for you to be all that you can be. Waiting for you to step on to the platform of this universe, the stage of the world to possess it all. To be everything that you were predestined to be even before the foundation of the world. Before you were conceived and formed in your mother's womb...yeah that thing! That place of being, that place of hope, yes, that place of being.

You must not forget that there are fundamental principles, basics to manifesting your goals, dreams, hopes and desires. Fundamental things that we cannot go around, we must endure. We must endure. We must endure.

See, the posture of our wait is so important. The posture of our wait is so important. The posture of our wait is so incredibly important. When you go through, are you growing through? Are you faking it, until you make it, or are you being great where you are? As you are developing and growing into who you were destined to be. No need to fake it, greatness is already in you! The you is me, and the me is you.

Everything that I am putting out, I take in. I've had time to do the inner work. The inner work is the mental work that is required. Time to be set aside, to be set apart, to be "worked, worked, worked, worked, worked." Yes, I have. Things that I did not understand, that I could have internalized and allowed to be the detriment of me and everything that my mom persevered for over the course of the 9 months she carried and labored for me. I could not allow that to be in vain. Today, I am still standing, walking into the greatness that God, only God could allow to be so. So, when you start your journey, journey towards purpose and greatness, keep going. One day you'll look up and you'll be so much farther than the place where you first started.

The Wealthy Place MANIFESTO

My (The) Wealthy Place is a place where I am no longer held captive to my own way of thinking, feeling, acting and most of all "my will" rather I am totally and wholeheartedly yielded to the Will of My Lord & Savior Jesus Christ, the author and the finisher of my faith. My mind (mindset) is renewed, I stand on His Word, Lean-in to His purpose for me, I am motivated, my Faith is activated and strengthened, I STAY in position, STAY inspired, STAY connected and am confident in WHO I am and WHOSE I am.

God has purposed and positioned me for such a time as this to be His mouthpiece, oracle and vessel in the earth. He has called, qualified and established me according to His Word in 1 Peter 5:10 to do the work He has placed in my hands to do. The people, resources and networks needed to accomplish this work will fall into place as God directs, leads and guides me. The strategic plan by which I am to fulfill His will and purpose for my life in the earth will unfold and I shall MOVE from My Reality to MY Wealthy Place in Him.

My faith is so strong. I can SEE it. I can FEEL it. I can TASTE it. People around the world are awaiting my entrance to the nation's stage and I will walk into the destiny God, the Lord Jesus Christ has called me to. I shall be STEADFAST, UNMOVEABLE and ALWAYS ABOUNDING in the works of the Lord for as much as I know, MY labor is not in vain in the Lord. For the Lord of host is with me and the God of Jacob is MY REFUGE!

Seven (7) *Self-care Notes to ELEVATION*

As you embrace this declaration and embark on this journey to MOVE from your REALITY to your WEALTHY Place I want to leave you with **"Seven (7) *Self-care Notes to ELEVATION.*"** I believe that these self-care notes are the fundamentals of manifesting one's wealthy place.

Self-Care Note #1:
STOP Taking Yourself So Seriously

Get over YOU! It's NOT about YOU! Even though you are going through it—whatever "it" is for YOU. ***Don't YOU dare Stop, someone's watching YOU! – Your next level is not for you! It's for your neighbor—the person beside you, the person behind you...DON'T BE SELFISH!*** I admit that sometimes I've been so tasked oriented and focused on getting things (the job) done that I've forgotten or missed out on the simple things in life...the little things that count...RELAX enjoy the ride (the process)! If we change our perspective and mindset in the process it helps us to endure and grow through every encounter a lot easier.

I will climb up to my watchtower and stand at my guard post. There I will wait to see what the LORD says and how he will answer my complaint.

Habakkuk 2:1 (NLT)

_____

_____

_____

_____

_____

_____

_____

_____

_____

_____

_____

_____

_____

Self-Care Note #2:
Rest in Him

He's got it all under control.
Be…available…still and know. *God has a formula for our lives. Don't become distracted by the division and subtraction. He's setting you up to multiply and add unto you your heart's desire.* His Promises are Yes and Amen. Even in moments that you feel depleted, know that you are right where God would have you to be. He has the ultimate set-up! Sit back, Relax and commit to doing whatever it takes. *If you don't let it break you, the doors will swing open.*

"For I know the thoughts that I think toward you, saith the LORD, thoughts of peace, and not of evil, to give you an expected end."

Jeremiah 29:11 (KJV)

_____

_____

_____

Self-Care Note #3:
Choose to BELIEVE and NOT Doubt

Have FAITH (Fear Anchored In The Holy Ghost). Fear cannot stand in the same atmosphere of faith. Where faith takes root belief grows, when belief grows the manifestation of visions and dreams spring up in the earth. When I have faith I am no longer complaining. Complaining camouflages fear.

⁴ There is a river, the streams whereof shall make glad the city of God, the holy place of the tabernacles of the most High.
⁵ God is in the midst of her; she shall not be moved: God shall help her, and that right early.

Psalm 46:4-5 (KJV)

_____

_____

_____

_____

_____

_____

Self-Care Note #4:
SPEAK LIFE- DECLARE & DECREE
with Your 👄

I shall live and not die! I am MORE than a conqueror! I am the Apple of my father's eyes! I am the head and not the tail. Above and not beneath. AFFIRM these things in your spirit while also speaking them into the atmosphere. Speak life. ***Whether I'm on the mountain top or the valley below—FAVOR finds me wherever I go.***

Death and life are in the power of the tongue: and they that love it shall eat the fruit thereof.

Proverbs 18:21 (KJV)

_____

_____

_____

_____

_____

_____

Self-Care Note #5:
Eliminate All Other Options

MEANING...All other options NOT to live YOUR best life! When you have a passion and deep routed desire...NOT ONLY Dreaming, but DARE to ACT on YOUR DREAMs. It's in that moment that NOTHING ELSE REALLY MATTERS! REMOVE the Word "try" from Your vocabulary. Affirm, ALL I DO IS WIN!!! I'm a winner! I live life in the winners zone! COMMIT TO DO THE WORK! Perseverance is the Key! Miracles take place when YOU choose to believe and not doubt. The unveiling of greatness.

Trust in the LORD with all thine heart; and lean not unto thine own understanding. In all thy ways acknowledge him, and he shall direct thy paths.

Proverbs 3:5-6 (KJV)

_____

_____

_____

Self-Care Note #6:
It's not going to happen overnight!

Get it out of YOUR mind! Take daily steps to achieving YOUR goals! You owe this to YOU! Now, is your time. Make a MOVE. God is waiting to give you the desires of Your Heart. Get Up, Show Up & Go Up! Half the battle is in showing up. Don't worry about what the NEXT step will be, just make the first by making a conscious decision to Show Up! God has EVERYTHING else under control (Trust & Believe). By doing so you tell the universe that you are making your election sure! It's YOUR TIME, Now MOVE! *FOCUS—follow one's course until successful!*

Wait patiently for the LORD. Be brave and courageous. Yes, wait patiently for the LORD.

Psalm 27:14 (NLT)

_____

_____

_____

_____

Self-Care Note #7:
Just Do It! STOP Second Guessing Yourself.

At times we get caught up in whether or not we have the right words, language and/or even can articulate and flow in a "particular way". So much so, that we often compare ourselves to others as opposed to just going, moving and being who God has called and proclaimed us to be in the earth. Can YOU just GO? MOVE? Tap into that place, thing, idea, creation, invention God has given YOU? Remember, God gave it to you and NOBODY else can do what He's given you! There may be variations, but there are no duplications!!! Just GO!

God has entrusted YOU with a vision HE wants to birth out in the earth. It is in realizing that you have a responsibility in being a good steward over that which He has placed into your care. Write the vision, make it plain and run with it. Pursue with all of your might! Live life unapologetically. Be unapologetic ABOUT pursuing your PURPOSE! No more second guessing, talking and/or walking yourself out of the plan and will of God. God has given you instructions, the OK, green light and go ahead. Don't allow YOUR prayers, tears and rolling in the floor to go in vain. God has given YOU the answer, perhaps just enough for YOU to make the 1st MOVE, then you must be ALL in to TRUST Him for the steps that will follow.

For it is God who is producing in you both the desire and the ability to do what pleases him.

Philippians 2:13 (ISV)

_____

_____

_____

_____

_____

_____

_____

_____

_____

_____

_____

Wealthy Place Affirmations

I will BELIEVE and not doubt.
I will STAY in PURPOSE.
I will STAY in HOPE.
I will STAY in TRUTH.
I will STAY in LOVE.
I will STAY in STRENGTH.
I will STAY FOCUSED.
I will STAY CONNECTED.
I will STAY in FAITH.
I Will STAY INSPIRED.
I will STAY in POSITION.
I will BE STILL.
I will BE CONFIDENT.
I will BE CONSISTENT.
I will BE REAL.
I will BE TRUE.

Our Deepest Fear
By Marianne Williamson

"Our deepest fear is not that we are inadequate. Our deepest fear is that we are powerful beyond measure. It is our light, not our darkness that most frightens us. We ask ourselves, Who am I to be brilliant, gorgeous, talented, fabulous? Actually, who are you *not* to be? You are a child of God. Your playing small does not serve the world. There is nothing enlightened about shrinking so that other people won't feel insecure around you. We are all meant to shine, as children do. We were born to make manifest the glory of God that is within us. It's not just in some of us; it's in everyone. And as we let our own light shine, we unconsciously give other people permission to do the same. As we are liberated from our own fear, our presence automatically liberates others."

From Reality to a Wealthy Place

ABOUT THE AUTHOR

Mone't S. Horton inspires spirit-led aspiring and current entrepreneurs in fulfilling their life purpose. Ms. Horton, the purpose driven inspirational coach, speaker and psalmist is the Visionary and Chief Inspiration Officer (CIO) of *Mo's Enterprise* LLC which houses *Connecting the Pieces (CTP) Coaching & Consulting Solutions, Mo's Inspiration for You, Leading Ladies Women's Empowerment Network* and *Mo Fashions*.

She believes ***that all YOU need is within YOU—NOW, is the time to tap in!*** Through her own journey, she has learned to embrace the process of life, stay in position, tap into her inner strength and manifest! Spirit-led, she serves as a mouthpiece and vessel on a mission to change the lives of people within her reach, with a specific passion for empowering youth and women to manifest beyond their wildest dreams and imagination! ***Mone't helps you move from your REALITY to your WEALTHY PLACE!***

@mosenterprise

Mone't S. Horton

Inspirational Coach, Speaker, Psalmist, Spirit-Led Entrepreneur

Made in the USA
Columbia, SC
24 August 2017